Basketball

Contents	Page
What is basketball?	2-3
Skills	4-5
Rebounding	6
Passing	7
Defending	8
Start the game	9
Rules	10-11
Scoring	12-13
Competitions	14-15
Play the game	16

written by John Lockyer

Can you jump? Can you run forward and back? Can you pass, catch, and bounce a large ball? If you can do these things, then the wonderful world of basketball is at your fingertips.

People have played the game of basketball for hundreds of years. The first basketball was a soccer ball, and the first goals were fruit baskets. There were nine players in each team.

Basketball players must learn useful skills. Shooting is an important skill. Good players can shoot the ball into the basket from anywhere close to the goal. When they shoot, they must concentrate on the basket.

shooting

Another important skill is dribbling the ball. Dribbling is when players bounce the ball as they move up and down the court. Every player needs to dribble the ball at some time in a game.

Sometimes a player will miss a goal. When the ball bounces off the backboard, anyone can grab it. This is called rebounding. Lots of practice in jumping up helps players to become better rebounders.

There are many different basketball passes: chest pass, bounce pass, overhead pass and baseball pass. All passes on the court should be fast and straight.

Players are defending when they try to stop the players in the other team from scoring a goal. Stealing or taking the ball cleanly from another player is the best way to defend.

defending

Playing the game is the best fun, but there are rules. Each team has five players. The game starts with a tip-off. The referee throws the ball up, and one player from each team tries to tap it to a teammate.

The player who has the ball must dribble to move forward or back. But it is against the rules to dribble, pick up the ball, then start dribbling again. It must be passed to someone else.

dribbling

No player can hit, push, or charge into another player. This is called fouling. If a player is fouled when he is shooting, he gets extra shots. If a player gives six fouls, he must leave the game.

Players can score between one and three points for each goal. A free throw is worth one point. Free throws are given to players who have been fouled. A goal that is shot from in front of the three-point line gets two points.

free throw

Three points are scored from a goal that is shot from behind the three-point line. All the team's players help each other to shoot goals. When the game is over, the winning team is the one with the most points.

Basketball is played by some of the best players in the world. Some countries have special competitions for players called professionals, who are paid to play basketball for a job.

stadium

Their games are played in huge stadiums, where many people come to watch them play. Basketball is a fast and exciting game. The crowd always claps and cheers when the players do a slam dunk.

Basketball can be played at school, at home, in the gym or in the park. It's a great way to make friends. Get into the game!